The Philosophical Origins of Austrian Economics

David Gordon

The Ludwig von Mises Institute
Auburn University
Auburn, Alabama 36849-5301

Published by Praxeology Press of the Ludwig von Mises Institute, Auburn University, Auburn, Alabama 36849-5301.

Library of Congress Catalog Card Number: 93-083764

ISBN: 0-945466-14-5

The Philosophical Origins of Austrian Economics

The Austrian school of economics arose in opposition to the German Historical School; and Carl Menger developed his methodological views in combat with the rival group. I thus wish first to discuss the philosophical doctrines of the Historical School, since this will deepen our comprehension of the contrasting Austrian position.

This monograph was prepared from a transcript of a talk I gave at the Mises University summer program at Stanford University. The informal style of an oral presentation has been retained here. The text has been edited, expanded, and lightly documented.

Next, I shall examine some of the philosophical influences on the founders of the Austrian school, in particular Franz Brentano and his followers. Brentano was the leading Austrian philosopher of the late nineteenth century. He favored a return to Aristotle, and I shall be stressing the Aristotelian roots of the Austrian school.

Eugen Böhm-Bawerk, the second great figure of the Austrian school after Menger, was influenced by a quite different school of philosophy, the nominalists. I shall briefly examine his emphasis on conceptual clarity.

Ludwig von Mises, the greatest twentieth-century Austrian economist, found himself the target of philosophical attack. The logical positivist movement subjected his deductive or praxeological approach to severe scrutiny. The philosophers of the Vienna Circle argued that science was empirical. Deduction cannot give us new knowledge about the world, without the use of non-deductive premises. We shall examine the force of the positivist criticism.

Before beginning the discussion of the Austrians, I think it essential to note that in intellectual history it is normally quite difficult to establish who influenced a particular author. One can very often show parallels between doctrines, but except for special cases, one can usually attain to no more than a suggestive hypothesis. If an author states directly that he has been influenced by someone, one of course can go beyond guesswork; but, unfortunately, the thinkers we have here to consider were rarely explicit about their intellectual sources. The account presented below aspires at most to plausibility. No historical interpretation is apodictically true.

The German Historical School included among others, Adolf Wagner, Karl Knies, and Gustav Schmoller. Although most people think of the group as confined to the nineteenth century, it lasted substantially longer. Werner Sombart, the most important member of the younger Historical School, died in 1939. Sombart, incidentally, was a friend of Mises and the teacher of Ludwig Lachmann. Another economist, Othmar Spann, who was quite sympathetic to the Historical School, lived until 1951. For a short time, Spann was a teacher of Friedrich Hayek, but Hayek was expelled from Spann's seminar.

The Historical School's view of economics differed not only from the Austrian school but from classical economics as well. The members of the group rejected laws of economics, even such basic principles as the law of supply and demand. They regarded economics as a historical and practical discipline.

Somewhat in the manner of Aristotle, who characterized economics as the study of household management, they thought of economics as the science of state management. Here they continued the tradition of the German mercantilists of the seventeenth and eighteenth centuries, the so-called Cameralists. They were less interested in economic theory than in the advancement of the power of the state, particularly the Prussian state, or, after 1871, the German Empire of which Prussia was the principal constituent.

These views hardly sound as if they were based on philosophy. Nevertheless, as it seems to me, strong philosophical currents helped to produce the characteristic doctrines of the Historical School. In particular, the members of the school were to some extent influenced by the most influential and important German philosopher of the early nineteenth century, G. W. F. Hegel.

Hegel was quite well informed about economics. He read the British economists very carefully, including Adam Smith; Sir James Steuart was an especial favorite of his. He did not reject the market: quite the contrary, he thought that property and the right to engage in free exchange were very important constituents of a good society.[1]

Hegel considered the development of autonomy essential for each individual within society; in this respect at any rate, he did not diverge from Immanuel Kant. To become self-determining, a person needs to have property, through the development of which his personality will take shape. Further, he needs to make decisions. Exchange provides people with just the opportunities they require.[2]

Hegel cannot however be considered a supporter of the free market, whether in the full-fledged Austrian sense or in the more attenuated fashion of most American economists. Freedom of exchange exists within civil society, but civil society is subject to control by the state.

---

[1]Richard Dien Winfield, *The Just Economy* (New York: Routledge, 1988) discusses and defends Hegel's economic doctrines.

[2]Jeremy Waldron, *The Right to Private Property* (Oxford: Oxford University Press, 1988) elaborately analyzes Hegel's argument for private property.

In elaborating his conception of the proper order of society, Hegel made use of one of the most important of his philosophical doctrines. The view in question influenced the main successors of Kant—Johann Fichte and Friedrich Schelling as well as Hegel. It is usually called the doctrine of internal relations.

According to this principle, everything that exists is bound together in a tight unity. More exactly, if two substances stand in a relation, neither would be the same substance if the relation were altered. A relation generates a relational property that is part of the essence of its bearer.[3]

An example will perhaps make this clearer. Suppose that I do not know President Bill Clinton. If I were to meet him, I would remain the same person. Being unacquainted with Clinton is not part of my essence. So at least common sense has it.

The supporter of internal relations denies this. He thinks that all an entity's properties are essential to it. My meeting with President Clinton affects each of my other properties. The person

---

[3]Brand Blanshard, *Reason and Analysis* (La Salle, Ill.: Open Court, 1973), p. 475.

who has met the President is a different person from the one who has not, however similar the two otherwise are.

Further, the relations of every single substance cover the entire universe. Everything is related to everything else.

The doctrine of internal relations has drastic consequences for science. Since all things are connected, full knowledge of anything requires knowledge of everything. The characteristic method of economics proceeds through the use of theories or models. These consider a particular group of factors in isolation from the rest of the world.

Supporters of internal relations would consider this method illegitimate. To consider certain factors apart from all else is to ensure a misleading picture. Instead, the economist should come as close as he can to a total picture of everything related to the economy.

Thus, economics should not be sharply separated from other disciplines connected with society. It should be studied together with history, political science, ethics, etc. Each economic system exists as a concrete entity embedded in a particular society. There are no universal laws of economics since they presuppose that the economy can be studied separately from the rest of society. At most, economic laws are confined to particular types of society.

The view that the economy is tightly interlocked with other social institutions is an application of a category of Hegel's Logic: organic unity.[4] In an animal, the parts function in relation to one another, subordinated to the whole organism. This is exactly the way the economy works, according to the Historical School.

Hegel by no means thought that organic unity was the highest category. It was however as far as one could go in the sciences. Although I have concentrated the discussion of organic unity on economics, Hegel applied the notion very extensively elsewhere. In his rarely studied *Philosophy of Nature*, Volume II of the *Encyclopedia*, he criticized Sir Isaac Newton. Kant viewed Newton's physics as the ideal of knowledge; but to Hegel, Newton's theories suffered from a fundamental flaw. Newton sharply distinguished physics from

---

[4]For a defense of organic unity by a contemporary Hegelian, see Errol Harris, *The Foundations of Metaphysics in Science* (New York: Humanities Press, 1965), pp. 279–84.

other areas of knowledge: his system depended only on a stated set of assumptions. By contrast, Hegel praised Johannes Kepler, who tried to bring the laws of astronomy into correspondence with mystical doctrines about numbers.

Hegel attempted to apply in practice what he taught in theory. In his doctoral dissertation, he sought to show that necessarily the number of planets in the solar system was seven. The number of planets did not just happen to be seven: that would contradict the doctrine of internal relations. Shortly after the dissertation appeared, another planet was discovered, which rather upset matters. Nevertheless, Hegel never revised his view that all relations are necessary.

There is yet another part of Hegel's philosophy which bars the way to economic science. As economics and the other sciences today conceive of laws, they apply to the future as well as the past. For example, according to the law of demand, a rise in the quantity demanded of a commodity will result in a rise in its price, other things being equal. The law applies not only to past increases in demand but to future increases as well.

Hegel doubted whether the future was predictable, at least in important respects. The philosopher could only sum up the past: he could not reveal the future progress of absolute spirit. As he famously says in the preface to the *Philosophy of Right*, "the Owl of Minerva takes wing only with the coming of dusk."

One might object that Hegel himself, most notably in *The Philosophy of History*, did attempt to arrive at laws of historical development. Indeed, for just this reason Karl Popper has stigmatized him as a "historicist."[5] But in fact his view of history agrees exactly with the skepticism about the future just attributed to him.

Hegel's law of history as the growth of freedom was a description of the past. He did not attempt to forecast future developments. No doubt one can say that the future, whatever it turns out to be, will be governed by the World Spirit. It is also true that the final stage of the dialectic is the Absolute Idea coming to full self-consciousness. This does not however enable particular trends or events to be predicted.

The parallel here with the Historical School is apparent. Sombart and other members of the

---

[5]Karl Popper, *The Open Society and Its Enemies*, vol. II (New York: Harper, 1967), pp. 27–80.

Historical School also attempted to elucidate the stages of historical development. Their doing so was quite consistent with the rejection of universal laws.

The portrayal of Hegel's system attempted here must meet a strong objection. Granted that Hegel held philosophical positions, i.e., internal relations and inability to predict the future, which are inimical to a science of economics, it does not follow that he thought every science was governed by these assumptions. They are philosophical theories, not scientific ones.

It is certainly correct that Hegel's philosophy is not logically inconsistent with a science of economics. But to the extent that this philosophy came into general circulation, its fundamental assumptions tended to inhibit the growth of scientific economics. The evidence for this consists of the distinctive doctrines of the Historical School and their Hegelian parallels. The criticisms of the "method of isolation" by Sombart and others are particularly suggestive of the doctrine of internal relations.

One potentially misleading interpretation needs to be noted. I do not contend that the members of the Historical School considered themselves

Hegelian. After Hegel's death in 1831, his philosophy fell into eclipse. Nevertheless the fundamental assumptions of his thought were pervasive in German intellectual life.

The parallels between Hegel and the Historical School extend beyond philosophy. Specific economic doctrines professed by the school echo Hegel's views. A principal criticism that the Historical School directed against capitalism concerned the neglect of agriculture. By undue stress on economic efficiency, traditional methods of farming were in danger of falling into disuse. For that matter, agriculture might suffer an absolute decline, if market pressure induced farmers and workers to enter industry.

Gains in efficiency were of scant interest to the Historical School. Instead, agriculture was to them a backbone of society and needed to be preserved. Exactly the same position is found in Hegel's *Philosophy of Right*. Agriculture counts as an "estate" which is to be safeguarded: it receives representation as a corporate body in the legislature.

More generally, Hegel saw the state as the director of the economy. "Civil society," though not a part of the state, fell under its authority. To allow unrestricted scope to the supposed laws of classical economics was to subordinate a higher entity, the state, to a lower, the economy. Instead, the economy should be manipulated to enhance the state's power.

It is no accident, I suggest, that the Historical School favored precisely the same views. Mises in *Omnipotent Government* has described in detail the way in which German economists before World War I advocated the use of the economy as a means to advance the power of the state. Trade should not be free but controlled by the state for its own purposes.[6]

The Austrian School stood diametrically opposed to the German Historical School.[7] In view of the vast divergence of the two schools in economics, one might expect substantial differences in philosophical background. This is indeed what one does find. The leading philosopher who influenced Carl Menger was Franz Brentano.

---

[6]Ludwig von Mises, *Omnipotent Government* (New Haven: Yale University Press, 1944).

[7]The treatment of the German Historical School given above has been influenced by Ludwig von Mises, *The Historical Setting of the Austrian School of Economics* (1969; Auburn, Ala.: Ludwig von Mises Institute, 1984).

He resolutely rejected the doctrine of internal relations, along with the remainder of the Hegelian system.

Brentano, who was Professor of Philosophy at the University of Vienna during the latter part of the nineteenth century, was a colleague and friend of Menger. Brentano was for most of his adult life a Roman Catholic priest; but after a theological quarrel, he abandoned the Church and was forced to resign his professorship.

His scholastic training contributed to his strong interest in Aristotle. He held Kant and Hegel in contempt, viewing them as retrogressive figures. Most important for our present purpose, he rejected the doctrine of internal relations.

He did not believe that everything was so internally bound up with everything else that nothing could be studied separately. Quite the contrary, the mind was sharply distinct from the external world. Further, Brentano extended his analytical, dissective approach to the mind itself. He distinguished acts of consciousness from their objects.

Brentano's study of the mind, *Psychology from an Empirical Standpoint*, was probably his most famous philosophical work and makes a vital contribution to understanding the Austrian theory of value. Brentano in this work and in several smaller works applied his general notion of mind to the concept of value. His approach to mind overthrew the prevailing notion of the mental common to almost all philosophers since René Descartes. The position he was opposed to was especially characteristic of the British Empiricists.

Philosophers such as John Locke and David Hume held, to oversimplify, that ideas are pictures impressed on the mind by external objects. At least when in receipt of impressions, the mind is passive. The empiricists recognized active powers of the mind to some extent. But in order for the active powers to function, the mind first had to have ideas impressed on it. (Innate ideas are a complication that for our purposes can be ignored.)

The working of the mind in perception, according to Locke and Hume, was in essence automatic. If one saw a particular object, an idea would enter one's mind. The various ideas one accumulated were connected by laws of association. There was little room for the mind to operate in an autonomous fashion. Indeed, Hume denied that a separate idea of the self existed: all that he could locate was a stream of perceptions.

Brentano rejected altogether the position just sketched. The "ideas" of the empiricists did not in fact designate mental activities: rather, to the extent they existed at all, they were the objects of the mind's activity. If, for example, I think of a chair, my mental action is not a picture of the chair found in my mind. What my mind does is to think of an object. Thinking is an action, a mental "doing," as it were. Brentano's term for mental action was intentionality: in his famous slogan it is the "mark of the mental."

In view of the importance of intentionality, let us risk laboring the point. An intention is a mental going out or grasping an object: it can be diagrammed as an arrow going from mind to object.

In speaking of "object," I have been guilty of an ambiguity. An object of an intention can be either a mental object, e.g., the ideas of the empiricists, or a physical object. Does the intentional act extend "out of" the mind to make direct contact with the actual world? This is a difficult issue to answer, as Brentano's system is rather murky on the point.[8]

---

[8]Brentano's views are very well analyzed in David Bell, *Husserl* (London: Routledge, 1990).

Menger applied the concept of intentionality to economic value. He did not take value to be a feeling of pleasure or pain that comes into one's mind automatically when one perceives an object. Quite the contrary, a preference in Menger's system is a judgment: I like X (or I dislike X). The judgment in question is an *act* of preference: as the intentionality of thought grasps an object, so does a judgment of preference "move" toward an end. In slightly different terms, to prefer something is to evaluate it: to rank it on one's scale of values.

By contrast, William Stanley Jevons had an entirely different notion of value. He equated value with utility or pleasure, measurable in units. He thought that an object created a certain number of units of pleasure in a person's mind when he came into the appropriate form of contact with it. The person as such really has little to do in regard to evaluation. Whatever created more units of pleasure, a strictly objective matter, was *ipso facto* the more valuable.

Conventional histories of economics class Jevons and Menger together with Léon Walras as the co-creators of the "subjectivist revolution." But in fact Menger ought not to be placed in the same group as the other two. (Walras will not be discussed in detail here: he tended to take "value" as an arbitrary unit or numeraire.) Only Menger had the notion of value as a judgment, a view which mirrored Brentano's analysis of the topic.

Menger was of course not the only important Austrian to be influenced by philosophy. His disciple Eugen von Böhm-Bawerk also displayed philosophical themes in his work. Like Menger, he rejected the contention of the Historical School that there were no universally valid laws of economics. In an incisive essay, "Control or Economic Law," he criticized the claim that the state has the ability to secure a prosperous economy in sovereign disregard of economic laws. In taking this position, he implicitly rejected the position that all relations are internal; as we have already emphasized, this view precludes the possibility of scientific laws.

Unlike Menger, Böhm-Bawerk's principal philosophical inspiration was not Brentano, and through him Aristotle; it was instead the medieval philosopher William of Occam. The doctrine Böhm-Bawerk took over from Occam, however, was not exclusive to him but remained in the Aristotelian tradition.

The view in question was that concepts needed to be traced to their origins in perception, their ultimate source. If, e.g., Hegel refers to Absolute Spirit, an analyst in the tradition of Böhm-Bawerk would ask: where does this notion come from? Can one show how it might be arrived at through abstraction from experience? If one cannot, the concept should be rejected as meaningless.

As the issue will greatly concern us later, one point of clarification is here in order. Böhm-Bawerk did not hold that each concept must directly refer to something perceptible by the senses. Clearly, his source Occam would never have held such a view, since God is not perceptible and Occam was a devout Christian. Rather, the position is a more limited one. Concepts that do not refer to something perceptible must be derived from concepts of perceptible things.

By using this method of analysis, Böhm-Bawerk razed to the ground the confused efforts of the Historical School to describe the spirit of an age and to postulate "laws" unique to particular cultures. Böhm-Bawerk's aim in analysis was practical. He wished to know what scientific use could be made of concepts. In this way, though not in philosophical underpinning, his procedure resembled the quest in modern philosophy of science for operational definitions.

Böhm-Bawerk did not halt at the concept in his Herculean efforts to achieve clarity. He paid minute attention to the analysis of particular arguments advanced by other economists. By discovering logical errors in them, false doctrine would be overthrown and the cause of correct analysis advanced. The most famous instance of this procedure is his devastating examination of the economics of Karl Marx.

He devoted two main works to the criticism of Marx: a chapter in *Capital and Interest* and a separately issued pamphlet, *Karl Marx and the Close of His System*. By characteristically precise and detailed work, Böhm-Bawerk undermined the key principle of Marxist economics, the labor theory of value. Most famously, he showed that Marx was unable to explain prices of production by the use of labor prices. But characteristically, this was not enough for him. Although the difficulty just mentioned, the so-called transformation problem, sufficed to ruin Marxist economics, Böhm-Bawerk did not confine his discussion to this issue. He criticized virtually every sentence in Marx's derivation of his theory of value.

We have so far described the way in which philosophical ideas affected Menger's and Böhm-Bawerk's treatment of various issues within economic theory. But philosophy influenced them in broader issues as well. The Austrian view of method in economics manifests distinctive philosophical doctrines.

For one thing, both Menger and Böhm-Bawerk stressed very much that only individuals act, a position that once again put them in opposition to the Historical School with its Hegelian roots. According to the principle of methodological individualism, states, classes, and other collective entities are reducible to individuals in relations with one another. Statements such as "France declared war on Germany in 1870" are shorthand for statements about particular persons. This position may seem obvious: it appears strange to think of the state acting in a way not reducible to the actions of the people who compose it.

Nevertheless, during the late nineteenth century the point was by no means taken for granted. The Historical School rejected methodological individualism, and they were joined in this rejection by the foremost German legal historian of the period, Otto von Gierke. Even at a much later period, the Austrian economist Othmar Spann held similar holistic views.

Spann, who was briefly referred to earlier, thought that to consider individuals as separate actors was the height of folly. Individuals exist in relationships that form their characters. One must take these relationships as wholes incapable of further analysis. Few economists today hold such views, but the fact that they strike us as silly stems in part from the successful campaign for individualism by the Austrians.

What are the philosophical roots of methodological individualism? Here, I suggest, we must once more return to Aristotle. In the *Nicomachean Ethics*, he emphasizes individual human action. More speculatively, one can point to the role of individual substances in the *Metaphysics*, but the development of this point would take us too far afield.[9]

Another Aristotelian theme exercised great influence on the Austrians; and this one, fortunately, is easier to document. The characteristic method

[9]For an excellent brief introduction to Aristotle, see Henry Veatch, *Aristotle: A Contemporary Appreciation* (Bloomington: University of Indiana, 1974).

of Austrian economics, carried to its culmination in Mises, is deduction. One starts with a self-evident axiom ("man acts") and with the aid of a few subsidiary postulates, deduces the entire science of human action.

Where does this notion of science originate? Although, as earlier mentioned, it is very difficult in intellectual history to demonstrate direct influence, I think it is no accident that the idea of a deductive science is found in Aristotle's *Posterior Analytics*. Aristotle argues that a complete science must start with a self-evident axiom and, by the use of deduction, exfoliate the entire discipline. Often conditions force the use of mere empirical hypotheses, but this is a mere expedient. [10]

Empirical science exists as a placeholder for true science, which must work through deduction. When Brentano and others revived the study of Aristotle, this view of method became available for study in Austrian universities.

---

[10] Aristotle believed that through induction, one can arrive at true first principles. These form the basis of science. This is discussed in Terence Irwin, *Aristotle's First Principles* (Oxford: Oxford University Press, 1988), p. 35.

Aristotle also discusses the necessity of self-evident principles in the *Nicomachean Ethics*. He notes that to justify a proposition, one would normally proceed by citing another proposition. But if matters are left at this, the task is not finished. What in turn justifies the proposition advanced in support of one's original claim? Obviously, one can cite yet another proposition, but this procedure cannot continue forever.

One needs to start with one or more self-evident axioms from which justification proceeds. Unless this is done, reasons advanced in support of one's claims will hang in air. One will either pile up justifications indefinitely or argue in a circle. Once more the parallel with the Austrian procedure is precise. Praxeology stems from the axiom of action, which itself requires nothing further in its support.

A common mistake needs to be noted here. It does not follow from the regress argument about justification that one must always trace arguments to one axiom alone. All that the argument shows is that at least one self-evident principle is required to begin a chain of justification. But nothing in the argument limits the number of these principles.

If one were to argue that to avoid an infinite regress of justification, one must arrive at a single axiom, the argument would be fallacious. The argument, in brief, would be that since every proposition that is not self-evident requires justification, there must be some basic proposition which is the source from which all others are justified. This is equivalent to the "argument" that since everyone has a father, someone is everyone's father. Obviously, this is wrong.

When a proposition is claimed to be self-evident, this does not mean that one is appealing to a psychological experience of certainty in support of the proposition. To do so would precisely be not to claim that the proposition was self-evident, since its evidence here depends on something else—the psychological experience. Whether one has an "Aha" experience in the style of Gestalt psychology on coming to realize the self-evidence of a proposition is irrelevant.

The point is important because contemporary hermeneuticists sometimes maintain that the self-evident axioms of praxeology are really principles accepted by a particular community. This approach is just a variant of the psychological fallacy we have already considered. Whether a particular group accepts a proposition as an axiom differs from the question of whether the axiom is self-evident.

I have so far claimed that the deductive method of Austrian economics stems from Aristotle. But an obvious objection comes to mind. When one turns to the third great figure of the Austrian school, Ludwig von Mises, Aristotle seems absent from the scene. Instead, Mises resorts to a distinctively neo-Kantian terminology: in particular, he regards the propositions of Austrian economics as synthetic a priori truths. The action axiom assumes free choice, but this to Mises is but a postulate. Mises does not presume to legislate for the noumenal world. One cannot, he thinks, rule out the possibility that science will one day demonstrate that hard determinism is true. (Oddly, Mises here reverses Kant, who thought we were phenomenally determined but noumenally free.)

Having raised this objection, I shall not spend much time on it. Although Mises does indeed resort to Kantian language, nothing in his argument depends on Kant's system. As Mises employs the phrase "synthetic a priori proposition," for example, it simply designates a proposition that is necessarily true and not a tautology. Those who prefer an Aristotelian approach can easily translate Mises' terms into their own preferred usage.

Mises' chief importance for our purposes does not lie in his Kantian veneer. Rather, a group of philosophers, the logical positivists, who arose in the 1920s developed doctrines that threatened to undermine the Austrian system. Their views, to the extent they impinged on Mises' system, did not challenge his economics; it was instead his deductive method that roused the positivists to protest. For Mises, then, our focus is not on the philosophers who influenced him, but on those who attacked him. In his response to these attacks, Mises further developed and clarified the Austrian position.

The logical positivists or Vienna Circle met under the leadership of Moritz Schlick, a professor of philosophy at the University of Vienna. Although Schlick led the group, his own views were not in all respects characteristic of the Circle. As an example, he believed that ethics was a science, while most logical positivists regarded ethical assertions as empirically meaningless.[11]

---

[11]This position is the notorious "emotive theory of ethics."

Probably the most philosophically important member of the group was Rudolf Carnap, a German by birth but resident in Vienna. Ironically, Ludwig von Mises' brother, Richard von Mises, belonged to the Circle, as did Karl Menger, the son of the Austrian school's founder. Another member, Felix Kaufmann, was also a participant in Ludwig von Mises' seminar. Nevertheless, like all the members of the Circle, he strongly opposed Mises' deductive approach to economic method.

The group at its inception was not very influential. Eric Voegelin, who was in Vienna during the 1920s and 1930s, once told me in conversation that the logical positivists were usually regarded as eccentric and deranged. Voegelin's own negative view of the group perhaps colored his memory, but his testimony is nevertheless significant. The Circle became much more influential after the rise of Adolf Hitler to power in 1933. The European political situation, culminating in the German annexation of Austria in March, 1938, forced most of the logical positivists into exile. Many of them wound up in the United States and secured posts at major universities. It is largely owing to the logical positivist influence on American philosophy that most American economists reject praxeology. They regard Mises' method as old fashioned and scholastic, allegedly not in keeping with the dictates of scientific philosophy. The essence of logical positivism can for our purposes be quite simply stated. All empirical statements, i.e., statements about the world, must be testable. If a statement cannot be tested, then it has no empirical meaning. By "testable" or "verifiable" the positivists meant "capable of being perceived by the senses." This is the famous verifiability criterion of meaning, the Vienna Circle's most noted principle.

One can immediately see that the structure of Austrian economics is in deep trouble if the verifiability criterion is accepted. According to Mises, the propositions of economics are necessarily true. But necessary truths cannot provide information about the world, in the logical positivist view. Only propositions that can be both true and false, depending on circumstances, convey information. Propositions that either must always be true or must always be false do not. The conclusion then seems inescapable: Austrian economics conveys no information about the world.

The logical positivists did not deny that some propositions must be true. But, as suggested above, this lends no help to Austrian economics.

Logically necessary truths are just tautologies, i.e., statements that convey no new information about the world.[12] A prime example of tautology is a definition. In the classically trite example, the statement "a bachelor is a never-married male above a certain age" conveys no information about the world. It merely offers a definition. A definition tells us that two expressions can be substituted for each other in a sentence while preserving the truth value of the sentence. In like fashion, a necessarily false proposition is the negation of a tautology. If I were to claim that some bachelors are married, I would not be making a false assertion about reality. I would be misusing the expression "bachelor."

Has Austrian economics been dealt a crippling blow by these considerations? Mises certainly did not think so. In *The Ultimate Foundation of Economic Science*, he addressed the claim of Karl Popper that scientific propositions must be falsifiable. Although Popper was not a positivist, he intended his falsification criterion to separate scientific from non-scientific statements.

---

[12]J. Albert Coffa, *The Semantic Tradition From Kant to Carnap: To the Vienna Station* (Cambridge: Cambridge University Press, 1991) gives a comprehensive account of the logical positivists' philosophy.

Mises' comment was dismissive: "if one accepts the terminology of logical positivism . . . a theory or hypothesis is unscientific if it cannot be refuted by experience. Consequently, all a priori theories, including mathematics and praxeology are 'unscientific'. This is merely a verbal quibble."[13]

It is easy to see that Mises' reaction to the verifiability criterion would be the same. Praxeology arrives at truth by deduction. If someone wishes to define "meaning" so that the conclusions of praxeology are empirically meaningless, why should he care?

To this an obvious rejoinder suggests itself. The logical positivists did not view their criterion of meaning as an arbitrary proposal, to be dismissed by anyone not sharing the Circle's affinities. On the contrary, they claimed that their position was well supported. Are they correct?

I do not think so. In point of fact, the criterion is worthless, since every statement comes out verifiable under it. Suppose that "p" is a non-controversially verifiable statement, e.g., "there is a

[13]Ludwig von Mises, *The Ultimate Foundation of Economic Science*. (Kansas City: Sheed Andrews and McMeel, 1977), p. 70.

chair in this room." Let us take "q" to be a statement logical positivists reject as meaningless. A good example is one that Rudolf Carnap held up to ridicule when he called for an end to metaphysics. He cited the following from Martin Heidegger's *Being and Time* (1927): "The not nothings itself." I shall not attempt to explain this: one can see why Carnap presented it as a paradigm instance of a meaningless statement.

Does the verification principle eliminate it? Surprisingly, it does not. From p, we deduce p or q. (This step is non-controversial.) Assuming that a logical consequence of a verifiable proposition is itself verifiable, (p or q) is verifiable. Further, if p is verifiable, then the negation of p is verifiable; this principle seems difficult to question. Now, consider the statement [not-p and (p or q)]. This too is verifiable, by the application of our earlier results. Expanding, we get (not-p and p or q) is verifiable. P and not-p cancel out, giving the result that q is verifiable. Clearly, if the verification criterion cannot eliminate "the not nothings itself," it is not worth very much.

A falsification criterion fairs no better. If p is falsifiable, then (p and q) is falsifiable. Once more, not-p should be falsifiable if p is, though Karl

Popper has implausibly denied this. By an argument parallel with that for verification, we conclude that q is falsifiable.

One might think that this is a mere trick, readily avoidable through slight modification of the principle. There have been many attempts to formulate a criterion that comes up with the "right" results, but so far all have failed to withstand criticism.

Nevertheless, some people will persist in thinking that the principle is basically sound. To them, we can advance a deeper, if duller objection than the foregoing: why should one accept the verifiability criterion? Surely proponents of it owe us some argument that the statements they wish to eliminate as meaningless really are meaningless. They in fact do not provide any. Perhaps the best account of the criterion from a sympathetic point of view is found in Carl Hempel's *Aspects of Scientific Explanation* (1965). Hempel elaborately describes the modifications and complications of the criterion in the decades it has been discussed. But he offers no argument in its favor. Mises was entirely right. The verification principle is an arbitrary formulation that has no claim on our support.

Before leaving the verification principle, I should like to mention another criticism advanced against it. Many opponents of logical positivism contend that the criterion is self-refuting. It itself is neither analytic nor verifiable: Therefore, by application to itself, it is meaningless. The Polish phenomenologist Roman Ingarden was probably the first to advance this criticism, and it has been set forward very effectively by Hans Hoppe. I shall not discuss this objection in detail here: suffice it to say that if carefully handled the criticism strikes home.[14]

To my mind, the foregoing considerations dispose of logical positivism, at least for our purposes. Because of Karl Popper's great influence on contemporary economic methodology, however, I think it advisable to make a few remarks about his variant of positivism.

Popper has had some effect on Austrian economics, in large part owing to the fact that Friedrich Hayek, his close friend, has to some extent abandoned praxeology and adopted falsificationism.

[14]The criticism presupposes that the first argument given above can be escaped. Otherwise, the criterion *is* verifiable, since all statements are verifiable. The positivist will not find this "defense" to his liking.

In doing so, Hayek reemphasized a positivist strain in his thought which has been present since his university days. He has been deeply impressed by the physicist and philosopher Ernst Mach, whose views in many respects resembled logical positivism. Mach rejected concepts in physics which could not be derived from the senses. For example, he refused to accept Newton's doctrine of absolute motion because in his opinion it lacked empirical reference. He also rejected atomism: atoms did not really exist but were a mere hypothesis.

Hayek's Machian tendencies emerge in full force in *The Sensory Order*, his study of perception. Popper cannot be blamed or credited with Hayek's positivism. What he did was to help bring about Hayek's extension of positivism to economics.

But this has been a digression. To return to Popper, his basic doctrine modifies the verifiability criterion. Rather than say that a meaningful statement about the world must be empirically verifiable, Popper asserts that a scientific statement must be falsifiable. Popper utterly disclaims association with the positivists: he stresses that his falsification criterion is a test for scientific statements, not a criterion of meaning. At least in his earlier years, though, he set little store by non-scientific statements; and although he has in recent times grown increasingly willing to countenance "metaphysical" statements, he does not consider them true or false. Small wonder that Carnap and Herbert Feigl classed Popper as an ally.

To say that a proposition must be "falsifiable" instead of "verifiable" at first seems trivial. If a proposition is verified, its negation is falsified; if a proposition is falsified, its negation is verified. Consider, e.g., "The demand curve slopes downward and to the right." Whenever this is verified, its negation, "the demand curve fails to slope downward and to the right" is falsified.

Further, since any proposition is verifiable (as shown above), the negation of any proposition is falsifiable. But a proposition's negation is of course also a proposition. Its negation is then falsifiable. Since this negation is identical with the proposition from which we started, we conclude that any proposition is both verifiable and falsifiable.

What then is all the fuss about? Popper's falsification criterion is in fact much more than a triviality. He maintains that confirming a proposition does not add to the probability that it is true, since he rejects induction. No matter how many times a demand curve has been found to slope downwards and to the right, the chances that this statement is true have not gone up. Mises displayed characteristic good sense in having nothing to do with Popper's skepticism.

At every stage in the development of Austrian economics, philosophy has been an accompanying though not dominating presence. Action, that leitmotif of praxeology, has in the Austrian tradition received a distinctly Aristotelian analysis. Austrian economics and a realistic philosophy seem made for each other.

Bibliographical Essay

My discussion of the economic doctrines of the German Historical School relies mainly on two works by Ludwig von Mises: *The Historical Setting of the Austrian School of Economics* (Auburn, Alabama: Ludwig von Mises Institute, 1984) and *Omnipotent Government* (New Haven: Yale University Press, 1944). Erich Streissler contends that Mises' strictures on the German Historical School apply only to the later Historical School. The earlier Historical School was much more sympathetic to economic theory. See Streissler's essay in B. Caldwell, ed. *Carl Menger and His Legacy* (History of Political Economy, Annual Supplement to Volume 22, Durham, N.C.: Duke University Press, 1990), pp. 31–68. "The Influence of German Economics in the Work of Menger and Marshall" (Glencoe, Ill.: Free Press, 1951).

As for Werner Sombart, see the discussion by Mortin J. Plotnick, *Werner Sombart and His Type of Economics* (New York: EcoPress, 1937). Sombart's approach may be sampled in his *The Jews and Modern Capitalism* (New York: EcoPress, 1962) and

The Quintessence of Capitalism (London: T. F. Unwin, Ltd., 1915). These combine a vast amount of historical data with little analysis. Sombart wound up as a supporter of Hitler: see *A New Social Philosophy* (Princeton: Princeton University Press, 1937).

Very little of Othmar Spann is available in English; but his *History of Economics* (New York: Norton 1930) makes clear how strongly he was influenced by German Romantic thought, especially by Adam Mueller. Hegel's relation to Romanticism is a complicated issue not discussed in this essay. For an important treatment, the chapter "Expressionism" in Charles Taylor, *Hegel* (Cambridge: Cambridge University Press, 1975) should be consulted. Lewis Hinchman, *Hegel's Critique of the Enlightenment* (Gainesville: University Presses of Florida, 1984) is also excellent.

For Hegel's study of economics, Laurence Dickey, *Hegel: Religion, Economics and the Politics of Spirit 1770-1807* (Cambridge: Cambridge University Press, 1987) is a very thoroughly documented account. It stresses Hegel's attempt to adjust his religious and philosophical beliefs to his economic and historical investigations.

On the doctrine of internal relations, H. H. Joachim, *The Nature of Truth* (Oxford: Clarendon Press, 1906) presents a strong defense of the theory. G. E. Moore "Internal and External Relations" in his *Philosophical Studies* (New York: Harcourt, Brace, 1922) is a very important criticism. Moore contends that the internal relations view rests on a fallacy: To say that something will be different if it lacks any property that it in fact has is a trivial truth. It does not follow that a thing without any of its relational properties would be some other thing. Brand Blanshard, *Reason and Analysis* (La Salle, Ill.: Open Court, 1973), upholds the doctrine against all detractors.

The doctrine of internal relations is closely related to the notion of organic unity. On organic unity in Hegel's philosophy, one of the best treatments is by J.M.E. McTaggart, a philosopher of outstanding merit in his own right. See his *Studies in the Hegelian Dialectic* (Cambridge: Cambridge University Press, 1922) and *Studies in Hegelian Cosmology* (Cambridge: Cambridge University Press, 1901). I should warn the reader that my admiration for McTaggart as a commentator on Hegel is not universally shared.

A strong defense of Hegel's use of organic unity

by a writer thoroughly familiar with modern logic is Errol Harris, *Formal, Transcendental, and Dialectical Logic* (Albany, N.Y.: State University of New York Press, 1987). I reviewed this work in *International Philosophical Quarterly* 30 (December 1990): 503–507. Harris responded in "Reply to Gordon: Formal and Dialectical Logic," *International Philosophical Quarterly* 31 (1991); not to be outdone, I answered in "Reply to Harris: On Formal and Transcendental Logic," *International Philosophical Quarterly* 32 (1992). This exchange covers a number of the main issues in dispute between proponents of an "organic" approach to logic and their opponents. Harris's excellent *Cosmos and Anthropos* (Atlantic Highlands, N. J.: Humanities Press, 1991) should also be consulted for its Hegelian analysis of science.

As mentioned in the text, Karl Popper offers a contrasting interpretation of Hegel's philosophy of history from the one I favor. In his *The Poverty of Historicism* (New York: Harper, 1964), he attempted to demonstrate that we cannot "predict the future course of history" (p. vii). In my opinion, his argument fails: it relies on an equivocation in "future results of science." Nevertheless, the book is highly recommended. By far the best work about Hegel's influence on nineteenth century German philosophy is John Toews, *Hegelianism*

(Cambridge: Cambridge University Press, 1980). Herbert Marcuse assesses Hegel's influence from a "left-Hegelian" standpoint in *Reason and Revolution: Hegel and the Rise of Social Theory* (Boston: Beacon Press, 1960). Although the book has some valuable insights, its constant repetition of "the power of negative thinking" in Hegel is little short of obsessive. Karl Löwith, *From Hegel to Nietzsche* (New York: Anchor, 1967) is a work of deep learning.

Hegel's work on politics and economics has in recent years aroused enormous interest. William Maker, ed. *Hegel on Economics and Freedom* (Macon, Ga.: Mercer University Press, 1987) presents a number of different interpretations. One of the most interesting contributions to the volume is by Richard Dien Winfield; in his *Reason and Justice* (Albany, N.Y.: State University New York Press, 1988) he presents a full-scale defense of Hegelian economics. Although Winfield is not a full supporter of the free market, he sympathizes with capitalism much more than is customary among contemporary Hegelians; and he develops some excellent criticisms of Marx. Harry Brod, *Hegel's Philosophy of Politics* (Boulder, Colo.: Westview Press, 1992) claims that Hegel offers a "middle way" between liberalism and Marxism. Steven Smith, *Hegel's Critique of Liberalism* (Chicago: University of Chicago Press, 1989) is a very carefully crafted book. George Armstrong Kelly, *Hegel's Retreat from Eleusis* (Princeton: Princeton University Press, 1978) contrasts Hegel with later political thinkers.

Although in the text I could do no more than mention "civil society," the reader should be aware that this has become a very "hot topic" in contemporary political philosophy. A gigantic work on the subject is Andrew Arato and Jean Cohen, *Civil Society and Political Theory* (Cambridge, Mass.: MIT Press, 1992). Another large-scale volume, like Cohen and Arato written from a socialist viewpoint, is John Keane, *Democracy and Civil Society* (London: Verso, 1988). Z. A. Pelczynski, ed., *The State and Civil Society: Studies in Hegel's Political Philosophy* (Cambridge: Cambridge University Press, 1984) generally defends Hegel against the charge of supporting an all-powerful state. Norbert Waszek, *The Scottish Enlightenment and Hegel's Account of 'Civil Society'* (Boston: Kluwer, 1988) is valuable not only for the topic announced in its title but also for Hegel's study of the classical economists.

When we move from Hegel to Brentano, in my opinion the philosophical atmosphere changes for the better. Brentano's major work is available in English translation: Franz Brentano, *Psychology from an Empirical Standpoint*, trans. A.C. Rancurello et al., (London: Routledge, 1973). Brentano's discussion of "correct" and "incorrect" value judgments is in *The Origin of Our Knowledge of Right and Wrong*, R. M. Chisholm and Elizabeth Schneewind, trans., (Atlantic Highlands, N. J.: Humanities Press, 1969). G. E. Moore reviewed Brentano's value theory in *International Journal of Ethics* Vol. 14 (1903), pp. 115–123. Brentano's belief in the objectivity of values heavily influenced Moore and, for a time, Bertrand Russell as well. Thomas L. Carson, *The Status of Morality* (Dordrecht: D. Reidel, 1984) defends a Brentanist value theory. Ludwig von Mises was of a different mind on this topic: in *Theory and History* (New Haven: Yale University Press, 1957), p. 36, n.1, he rejects Brentano's theory. Unfortunately, Mises did not discuss Brentano's arguments. Brentano's doctrine of intentionality, probably his key contribution to philosophy, is discussed in detail in David Bell, *Husserl* (London: Routledge, 1990).

Locke's and Hume's views on the theory of knowledge are, I fear, grossly oversimplified in the text. For a correction, see H. H. Price, *Hume's Theory of the External World* (Oxford: Clarendon,

1940). This work shows how Hume built up a world out of sense-data: it is a beautifully written book and a personal favorite. Very different interpretations of Hume's epistemology from Price's, whom I follow in the text, are given by John Wright, *Hume's Skeptical Realism* (Manchester: Manchester University Press, 1983) and Galen Strawson, *The Secret Connexion: Causation, Realism and Hume* (Oxford: Oxford University Press, 1989). Michael Ayres, *Locke, Volume I: Epistemology* (London: Routledge, 1991) is by far the best book on Locke's theory of knowledge. Along with its companion volume *Ontology*, it is a major philosophical treatise. Ayres defends Lockean positions against many currently fashionable views.

I am not aware of any comprehensive account of W. S. Jevons's philosophy. His own most important work on the theory of knowledge is *The Principles of Science* 2 vols. (London: MacMillan, 1874). His views on utility are in *The Theory of Political Economy* (London: MacMillan, 1871). A vital work for understanding nineteenth century British empiricism is John Skorupski, *John Stuart Mill* (London: Routledge, 1989). Skorupski defends many of the characteristic theories of the empiricists. A very useful book that contrasts the British empiricists with the German Romantics in the theory of knowledge is Hans Aarsleff, *From Locke to Saussure* (Minneapolis: University of Minnesota Press, 1982).

As suggested in the text, Böhm-Bawerk's criticism of Marx provides one of the best examples of his analytical method. Later criticism of Marx's labor theory of values owes much to Böhm-Bawerk, as can be seen from one of the best summaries of recent work on the theory: Jon Elster, *Making Sense of Marx* (Cambridge: Cambridge University Press, 1985). In my *Resurrecting Marx* (Rutgers: Transaction Books, 1990), I discuss Böhm-Bawerk's arguments in more detail than here.

Methodological individualism is of course one of the key doctrines of Austrian economics. Alan Garfinkel, *Forms of Explanation* (New Haven: Yale University Press, 1981) is an important discussion but does not accept the individualist position. J. W. N. Watkins, "Ideal Types and Historical Explanation" in Alan Ryan, ed., *The Philosophy of Social Explanation* (Oxford: Oxford University Press, 1973) defends methodological individualism; so does, Jon Elster, in *Making Sense of Marx*, *op. cit.* Oddly, Elster claims that Marx was a methodological individualist. Margaret Gilbert, *On Social Facts* (London: Routledge, 1989) works out an original position on the issue: she argues that social phenomena involve "plural subjects." See also Robert Nozick, *The Examined Life* (New York: Simon and Schuster, 1989, p. 73).

Terence Irwin, *Aristotle's First Principles* (Oxford: Oxford University Press, 1988) is an extraordinarily detailed guide to Aristotle's views on proper method in philosophy and science. Irwin's notions of "weak and strong dialectic" are especially useful in understanding Aristotle. Two of the best recent discussions of the *Nicomachean Ethics* are Sarah Broadie, *Ethics with Aristotle* (Oxford: Oxford University Press, 1991) and Richard Kraut, *Aristotle on the Human Good* (Princeton: Princeton University Press, 1989). Douglas Rasmussen and Douglas Den Uyl, *Liberty and Nature* (La' Salle, Ill.: Open Court, 1991) applies Aristotelian insights to modern political philosophy. For a discussion of Aristotelian and Austrian economics, Barry Smith, "Aristotle, Menger, Mises: An Essay in the Metaphysics of Economics" in B. Caldwell, *op. cit.* (pp. 263–88) is essential reading.

My remark on p. 23 about self-evident propositions derives from G. E. Moore, *Principia Ethica* (Cambridge: Cambridge University Press, 1903). Michael Williams, *Groundless Belief* (Oxford: Oxford University Press, 1977) argues against self-evident propositions. For the viewpoint of hermeneutics, see the chief work of this school: Hans-Georg Gadamer, *Truth and Method* (New York: Seabury Press, 1975).

My assertion that Mises did not rule out determinism (p. 23) may appear surprising, but it is actually an understatement. Mises *was* a determinist: he thought however that science was not now in a position to discover the laws by which human thought operates. Hence a space exists for praxeology, a discipline that takes human beings to be rational actors. See *Theory and History*, *op. cit.* For an excellent account of Kant's philosophy, see Paul Guyer, *Kant and the Claims of Knowledge* (Cambridge: Cambridge University Press, 1987). Mises' remarks about categories of human thought do not involve him in Kant's complex arguments.

According to J. Alberto Coffa, *The Semantic Tradition from Kant to Carnap* (Cambridge: Cambridge University Press, 1991), the logical positivist philosophy arose in opposition to Kant's claim that a priori knowledge is based on pure intuition. The most famous account of the positivists' verification principle is A. J. Ayer, *Language, Truth and Logic*, rev. ed. (Oxford: Oxford University Press,

1946). The revised edition of the book should be consulted for Ayer's reformulation of the principle in response to criticism. To the end of his life, Ayer upheld the principle: see his "Reply to Dummett" in Lewis Hahn, ed., *The Philosophy of A. J. Ayer* (LaSalle, Ill.: Open Court, 1992), pp. 149–156. Michael Dummett's essay in the same volume, "The Metaphysics of Verificationism," pp. 129–148, should also be consulted. My criticism in the text of the positivist view of meaning owes a great deal to Alvin Plantinga, *God and Other Minds* (Ithaca, N.Y.: Cornell University Press, 1967).

I claim in the text that Karl Popper's view of meaning is no better than that of the positivists. For a vigorous argument to the contrary, see W. W. Bartley, III, *Unfathomed Knowledge, Unmeasured Wealth* (La Salle, Ill.: Open Court, 1990). His "critical rationalism" seems to me to allow one to believe whatever one chooses: the criticism to which beliefs are subjected rests on arbitrary standards.

Bibliography

Aarsleff, Hans. *From Locke to Saussure*. Minneapolis: University of Minnesota Press, 1982.

Arato, Andrew and Jean Cohen. *Civil Society and Political Theory*. Cambridge, Mass.: MIT Press, 1992.

Ayer, A. J. *Language, Truth and Logic*. Rev. Ed. Oxford: Oxford University Press, 1946.

Ayres, Michael. *Locke, Volume I: Epistemology*. London: Routledge, 1991.

Bartley, W. W., III. *Unfathomed Knowledge, Unmeasured Wealth*. La Salle, Ill.: Open Court, 1990.

Bell, David. *Husserl*. London: Routledge, 1991.

Blanshard, Brand. *Reason and Analysis*. La Salle, Ill.: Open Court, 1973.

Brentano, Franz. *The Origin of Our Knowledge of Right and Wrong*. Trans. R. M. Chisholm and Elizabeth Schneewind. Atlantic Highlands, N. J.: Humanities Press, 1969.

———. *Psychology from an Empirical Standpoint*. Trans. A. C. Rancurello, et al.London: Routledge, 1973.

Broadie, Sarah. *Ethics with Aristotle*. Oxford: Oxford University Press, 1991.

Brod, Harry. *Hegel's Philosophy of Politics*. Boulder, Colo.: Westview Press, 1992.

Coffa, J. Alberto. *The Semantic Tradition from Kant to Carnap*. Cambridge: Cambridge University Press, 1991.

Carson, Thomas L. *The Status of Morality*. Dordrecht: D. Reidel, 1984.

Coffa, J. Albert. *The Semantic Tradition from Kant to Carnap: To the Vienna Station*. Cambridge: Cambridge University Press, 1991.

Dickey, Laurence. *Hegel: Religion, Economics and the Politics of Spirit 1770–1807*. Cambridge: Cambridge University Press, 1987.

Dummett, Michael. "The Metaphysics of Verificationism." In *The Philosophy of A. J. Ayer*. La Salle, Ill.: Open Court, 1992, pp. 129–148.

Elster, Jon. *Making Sense of Marx*. Cambridge: Cambridge University Press, 1985.

Garfinkel, Alan. *Forms of Explanation*. New Haven: Yale University Press, 1981.

Gadamer, Hans-Georg. *Truth and Method*. New York: Seabury Press, 1975.

Gilbert, Margaret. *On Social Facts*. London: Routledge, 1989.

Gordon, David. "Review of Harris: On Formal and Transcendental Logic." *International Philosophical Quarterly* 30 (December 1990).

——. "Reply to Harris: On Formal and Transcendental Logic." *International Philosophical Quarterly* 32 (1992).

——. *Resurrecting Marx*. Rutgers, N. J.: Transaction Books, 1990.

Guyer, Paul. *Kant and the Claims of Knowledge*. Cambridge University Press, 1987.

Harris, Errol. *Cosmos and Anthropos*. Atlantic Highlands, N. J.: Humanities Press, 1991.

——. *Formal, Transcendental, and Dialectical Logic*. Albany, N. Y.: State University of New York Press, 1987.

——. *The Foundations of Metaphysics in Science*. New York: Humanities Press, 1965.

——. "Reply to Gordon: Formal and Dialectical Logic." *International Philosophical Quarterly* 31 (1991).

Hahn, Lewis, ed. *The Philosophy of A. J. Ayer*. La Salle, Ill.: Open Court, 1992, pp. 149–156.

Hempel, Carl. *Aspects of Scientific Explanation and Other Essays*. New York: Free Press, 1965.

Hinchman, Lewis. *Hegel's Critique of the Enlightenment*. Gainesville: University Presses of Florida, 1984.

Hoppe, Hans-Hermann. *Praxeology and Economic Science*. Auburn, Ala.: Ludwig von Mises Institute, 1988.

Irwin, T. H. *Aristotle's First Principles*. Oxford: Oxford University Press, 1988.

Joachim, H. H. *The Nature of Truth*. Oxford, Clarendon, 1906.

Jevons, W. S. *The Principles of Science*. London: MacMillan, 1874.

——. The *Theory of Political Economy*. London: MacMillan, 1871.

Keane, John. *Democracy and Civil Society*. London: Verso, 1989.

Kelly, George Armstrong. *Hegel's Retreat from Eleusis*. Princeton: Princeton University Press, 1978.

Kraut, Richard. *Aristotle on the Human Good*. Princeton: Princeton University Press, 1989.

Löwith, Karl. *From Hegel to Nietzsche*. New York: Anchor, 1967.

Maker, William, ed. *Hegel on Economics and Freedom*. Macon, Ga.: Mercer University Press, 1987.

Marcuse, Herbert. *Reason and Revolution: Hegel and the Rise of Social Theory*. Boston: Beacon Press, 1960.

McTaggart, J. M. E. *Studies in Hegelian Cosmology*. Cambridge: Cambridge University Press, 1901.

——. *Studies in the Hegelian Dialectic*. Cambridge: Cambridge University Press, 1922.

Mises, Ludwig von. *The Historical Setting of the Austrian School of Economics*. [1969] Auburn, Ala.: Ludwig von Mises Institute, 1984.

——. *Human Action*. Chicago: Henry Regnery, 1966.

——. *Omnipotent Government*. New Haven: Yale University press, 1944.

——. *The Ultimate Foundation of Economic Science*. Kansas City: Sheed Andrews and McMeel, 1977.

David Gordon

——. *Theory and History*. New Haven: Yale University Press, 1957.

Moore, G. E. "Internal and External Relations." *Philosophical Studies*. New York: Harcourt, Brace, 1922.

——. "Review of Franz Brentano, *The Origin of Knowledge Right and Wrong*." *International Journal of Ethics* 14 (1903): 115–123.

——. *Principia Ethica*. Cambridge: Cambridge University Press, 1903.

Nagel, Ernst. *The Structure of Science*. New York: Harcourt, Brace, World, 1961.

Nozick, Robert. *The Examined Life*. New York: Simon and Schuster, 1989.

Pelczynski, Z. A., ed. *The State and Civil Society: Studies in Hegel's Political Philosophy*. Cambridge: Cambridge University Press, 1984.

Plantinga, Alvin. *God and Other Minds*. Ithaca, N. Y.: Cornell University Press, 1967.

Plotnick, Mortin J. *Werner Sombart and His Type of Economics*. New York: EcoPress, 1937.

Popper, Karl. *The Open Society and Its Enemies*. Volume II. New York: Harper, 1967.

——. *The Poverty of Historicism*. New York: Harper, 1964.

Price H. H. *Hume's Theory of the External World*. Oxford: Clarendon, 1940.

Rasmussen, Douglas and Douglas Den Uyl. *Liberty and Nature*. La Salle, Ill.: Open Court, 1991.

Rothbard, Murray N. *Ludwig von Mises: Scholar, Creator, Hero*. Auburn, Ala.: Ludwig von Mises Institute, 1988.

Skorupski, John. *John Stuart Mill*, London: Routledge, 1989.

Smith, Barry. "Aristotle, Menger, Mises: An Essay in the Metaphysics of Economics." In B. Caldwell, ed. *History of Political Economy* (History of Political Economy, Annual Supplement to Volume 22, Durham, N.C.: Duke University Press, 1990).

Smith, Steven. *Hegel's Critique of Liberalism*. Chicago: University of Chicago Press, 1989.

Sombart, Werner. *A New Social Philosophy*. Princeton: Princeton University Press, 1937.

———. *The Jews and Modern Capitalism*. New York: EcoPress, 1962.

———. *The Quintessence of Capitalism*. London: T. F. Unwin, 1915.

Strawson, Galen. *The Secret Connexion: Causation, Realism and Hume*. Oxford: Oxford University Press, 1989.

Streissler, Erich. "Carl Menger and His Legacy." In B. Caldwell, ed. *History of Political Economy* (History of Political Economy, Annual Supplement to Volume 22, Durham, N.C.: Duke University Press, 1990).

Taylor, Charles. "Expressionism." In *Hegel*. Cambridge: Cambridge University Press, 1975.

Toews, John. *Hegelianism*. Cambridge: Cambridge University Press, 1980.

Watkins, J. W. N. "Ideal Types and Historical Explanation." In *The Philosophy of Social Explanation*. Alan Ryan. ed. Oxford: Oxford University Press, 1973.

Waszek, Norbert. *The Scottish Enlightenment and Hegel's Account of 'Civil Society'*. Boston: Kluwer, 1988.

Williams, Michael. *Groundless Belief*. Oxford: Oxford University Press, 1977.

Winfield, Richard Dien. *Reason and Justice*. Albany, N. Y.: State University of New York Press, 1988.

Wright, John. *Hume's Skeptical Realism*. Manchester: Manchester University Press, 1983.

About the Author . . .

David Gordon is a senior fellow at the Ludwig von Mises Institute. He earned both his undergraduate and graduate degrees from the University of California at Los Angeles. His Ph.D. studies were in the area of intellectual history. He is the author of *Resurrecting Marx: The Analytical Marxists on Exploitation, Freedom, and Justice* and *Critics of Marxism*. He is currently working on an updated and revised version of Henry Hazlitt's bibliography, *The Free Man's Library*. His articles can frequently be found in such scholarly journals as *Analysis, British Journal of Political Science, Canadian Journal of Philosophy, Ethics, International Philosophic Quarterly, Journal of Libertarian Studies, Journal of Value Inquiry, Mind, Political Studies, Politics, Religious Studies, Social Philosophy & Policy*, and the *Review of Austrian Economics*.

About the Ludwig von Mises Institute . . .

Founded in October 1982, the Ludwig von Mises Institute is dedicated to the work of Ludwig von Mises and the advancement of Austrian economics. The Institute's board is chaired by Mrs. Ludwig von Mises. The founder and president is Llewellyn H. Rockwell. Professor Murray N. Rothbard, Mises's top American student, is vice president for academic affairs.

In six decades of teaching and writing, Professor Mises rebuilt the science of economics, and the defense of the free market and honest money, on a foundation of individual human action. From then on, Marxists, Socialists, and Keynesians might retain their positions of power in governments and universities, but they had been defeated in the intellectual battle.

Mises dedicated himself to scholarship and freedom. The Mises Institute pursues the same goals through an extensive program of:

- Publications, including the twice-annual *Review of Austrian Economics* edited by Murray N. Rothbard; the monthly *Free Market*; the *Austrian Economics Newsletter*; books; monographs; and occasional papers in theory and policy.

- Fellowships and assistantships for Misesian graduate students.
- The O. P. Alford, III, Center for Advanced Studies in Austrian Economics.
- Academic centers at Auburn University and the University of Nevada, Las Vegas.
- Teaching programs and seminars, including the annual summer "Mises University."
- Conferences on such subjects as the gold standard, the Federal Reserve, taxes, Marxism, Keynesianism, bureaucracy, socialism, egalitarianism, and the work of Ludwig von Mises and Murray N. Rothbard.
- The Henry Hazlitt Fund for Economic Journalism.
- Public policy work on the free market and gold standard.

For more information on the Institute's work, please write: the Ludwig von Mises Institute, Auburn University, Auburn, Alabama 36849-5301.

OTHER MONOGRAPHS
PUBLISHED BY THE
LUDWIG VON MISES INSTITUTE

An Introduction to Austrian Economics
by Thomas Taylor

**The Austrian Theory of the Trade Cycle
and Other Essays**
Edited by Richard M. Ebeling

The Case for the 100% Gold Dollar
by Murray N. Rothbard

Economic Calculation in the Socialist Commonwealth
by Ludwig von Mises

**Freedom, Inequality, Primitivism, and the Division of
Labor**
by Murray N. Rothbard

The Historical Setting of the Austrian School
by Ludwig von Mises

Liberty and Property
by Ludwig von Mises

Ludwig von Mises: A Personal View
by Ron Paul

Ludwig von Mises: An Annotated Bibliography
by David Gordon

Methodology of the Austrian School Economists
by Lawrence H. White

Murray N. Rothbard: A Scholar in Defense of Freedom
by David Gordon

Praxeology and Economic Science
by Hans-Hermann Hoppe

Praxeology and Understanding: An Analysis of the Controversy in Austrian Economics
by George A. Selgin

Toward a Reconstruction of Utility and Welfare Economics
by Murray N. Rothbard

Two Essays by Ludwig von Mises: Liberty and Property and Middle-of-the-Road Policy Leads to Socialism
by Ludwig von Mises

What Has Government Done to Our Money?
by Murray N. Rothbard